For Becki

When the Lord sovereignly designed
all things in eternity past, out of all the ages
He could have chosen, and out of all of the people
He could have ordained,
He elected you, in this life, to be mine.

Only God would've planned it that way!

ONLY GOD
Would've Planned It That Way!

SAINT LOUIS

Written by Todd Barsness   Illustrated by Shelly Hehenberger

If I would've planned out the Lord's passion week,

The throngs would be gathered and autographs they'd seek.

But the fickle-ish crowds would become a mad fray—

You see, only God would've planned it that way!

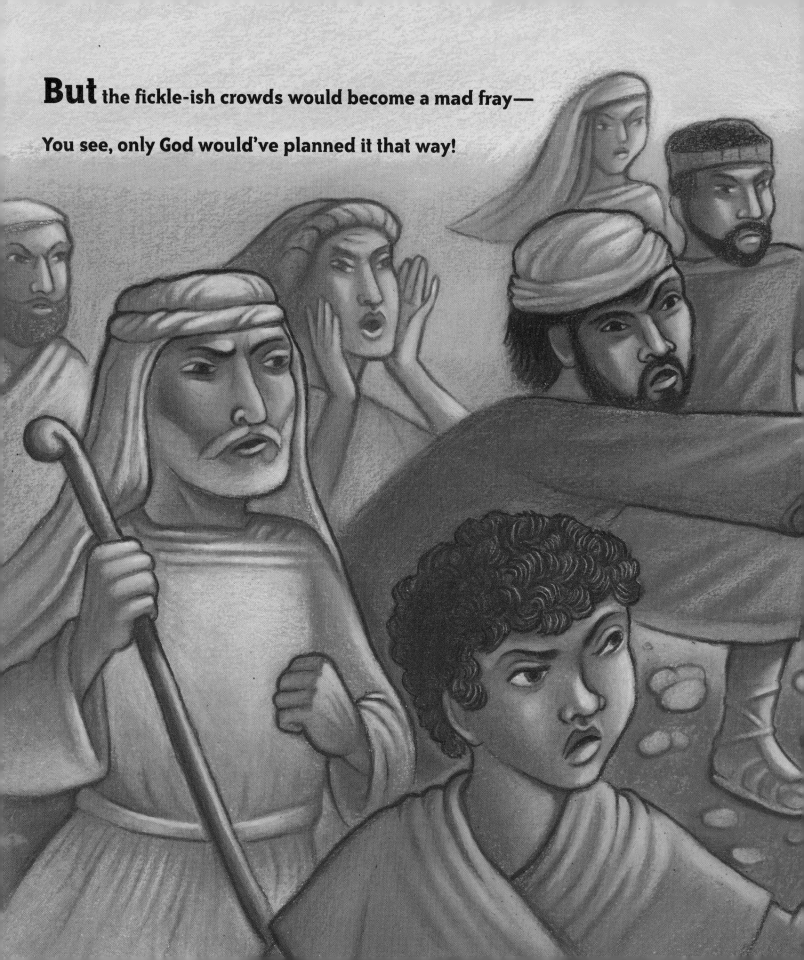

If I would've planned how a conqueror would ride,

I'd saddle a stallion with a big haughty stride.

Yet He hopped upon a small colt that spring day—

You see, only God would've planned it that way!

If I would've planned the last meal that He'd eat,

The best food and guests would be placed at His feet.

But He wept alone; in great sorrow He prayed—

You see, only God would've planned it that way!

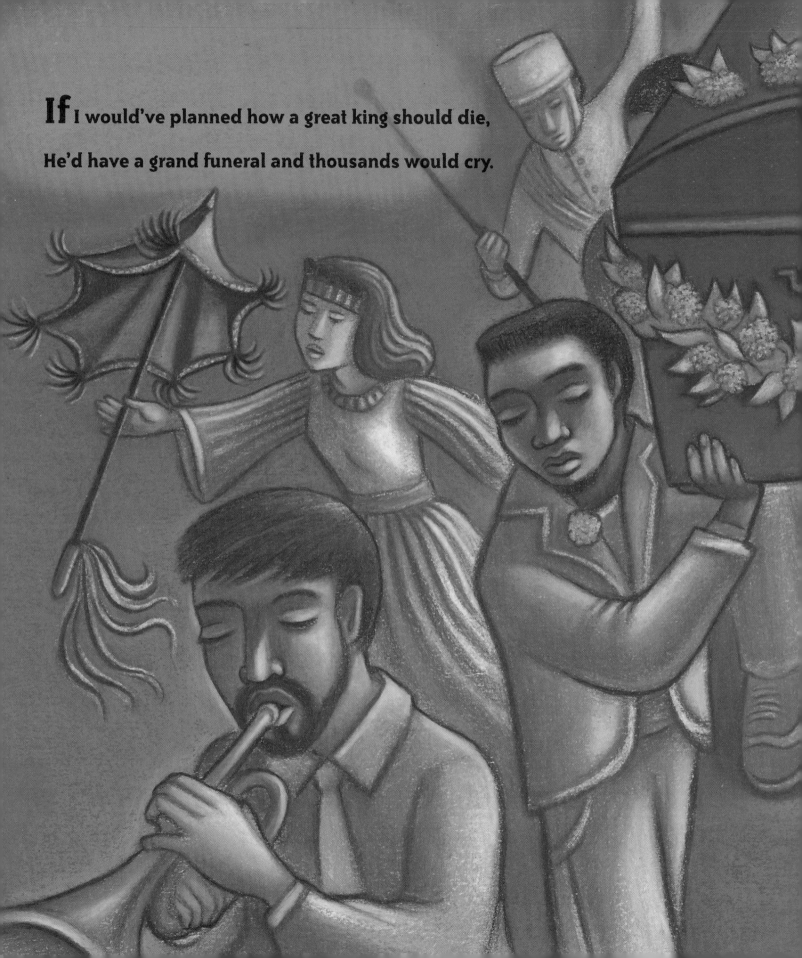

If I would've planned how a great king should die,

He'd have a grand funeral and thousands would cry.

But He hung on a cross on a day dark and gray—

You see, only God would've planned it that way!

If I would've planned the last statement He'd make,

I'd bring in reporters and notes they would take.

But "It is finished!" were the last words He'd say—

You see, only God would've planned it that way!

If I would've planned God's great love-plan for me,

I would not have sent Christ to die on that tree.

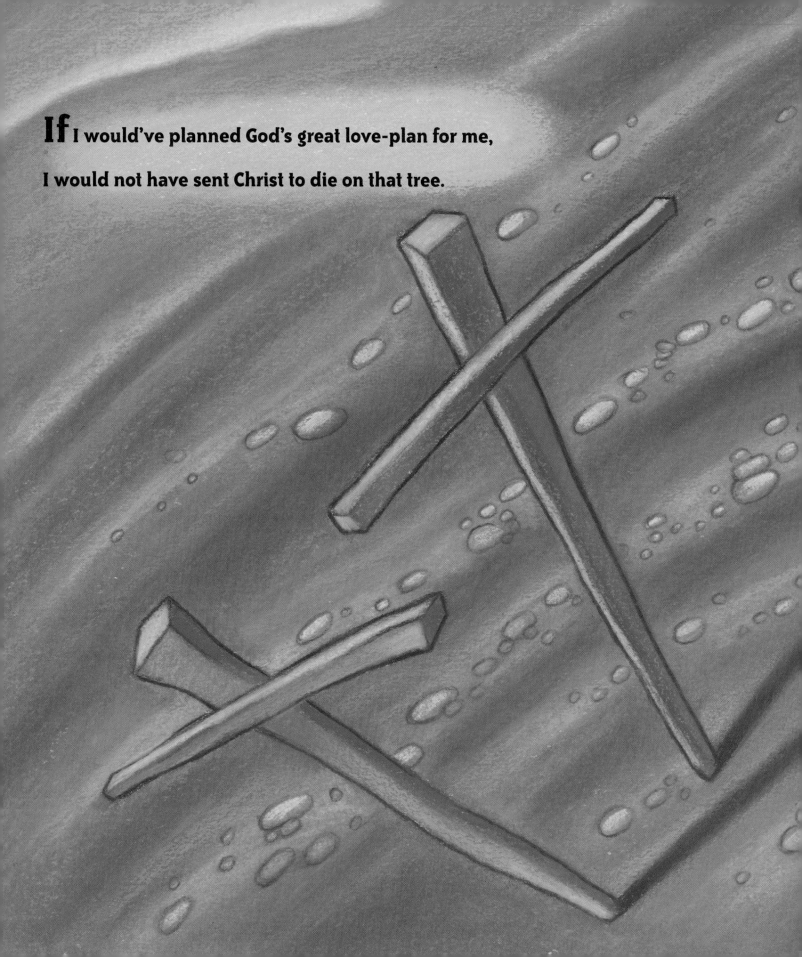

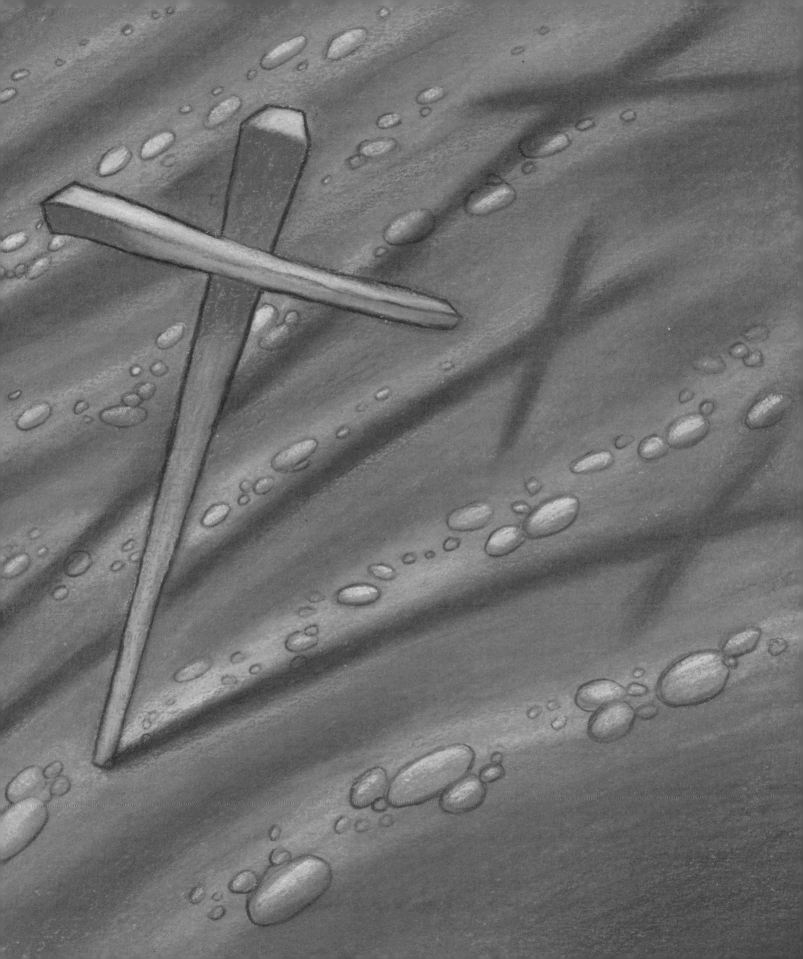

But God knew my sin needed infinite pay—

You see, only God would've planned it that way!

If I would've planned how Messiah would save,

He would not spend three days closed up in the grave.

But Christ rose from death that victorious day—

You see, only God would've planned it that way!

Text copyright © 2002 Todd Barseness
Illustrations copyright © 2002 Concordia Publishing House

Published by Concordia Publishing House
3558 S. Jefferson Avenue, St. Louis, MO 63118-3968
Manufactured in the United States of America

1 2 3 4 5 6 7 8 9 10   11 10 09 08 07 06 05 04 03 02